TEAM SPIRIT ®

SMART BOOKS FOR YOUNG FANS

THE TAMPA BAY BUCCANEERS

BY
MARK STEWART

New Hanover County Public Library
201 Chestnut Street
Wilmington, North Carolina 28401

NORWOODHOUSE PRESS

CHICAGO, ILLINOIS

Norwood House Press
P.O. Box 316598
Chicago, Illinois 60631

For information regarding Norwood House Press, please visit our website at:
www.norwoodhousepress.com or call 866-565-2900.

Editor: Mike Kennedy
Designer: Ron Jaffe
Project Management: Black Book Partners, LLC.
Special thanks to Topps, Inc.

Library of Congress Cataloging-in-Publication Data

Stewart, Mark, 1960-
    The Tampa Bay Buccaneers / by Mark Stewart.
        p. cm. -- (Team spirit)
    Includes bibliographical references and index.
    Summary: "A revised Team Spirit Football edition featuring the Tampa Bay
Buccaneers that chronicles the history and accomplishments of the team.
Includes access to the Team Spirit website which provides additional
information and photos"--Provided by publisher.
    ISBN 978-1-59953-541-8 (library edition : alk. paper) -- ISBN
978-1-60357-483-9 (ebook) 1. Tampa Bay Buccaneers (Football
team)--History--Juvenile literature. I. Title.
    GV956.T35.S74 2012
    796.332'640975965--dc23
                                                      2012020229

Manufactured in the United States of America in North Mankato, Minnesota.
205N—082012

COVER PHOTO: The Buccaneers celebrate a touchdown during the 2011 season.

Table of Contents

ABOUT OUR GLOSSARY

In this book, there may be several words that you are reading for the first time. Some are sports words, some are new vocabulary words, and some are familiar words that are used in an unusual way. All of these words are defined on page 46. Throughout the book, sports words appear in **bold type**. Regular vocabulary words appear in ***bold italic type***.

Meet the Buccaneers

There is an old saying in football that defense wins championships. Fans of the Tampa Bay Buccaneers won't argue with that. The "Bucs" have always been at their best when their defense leads the way. Their most famous players are known for hard tackles, key **interceptions**, and timely **sacks**.

Playing tough defense requires just as much skill and teamwork as scoring points on offense. In fact, often it takes even more. The Buccaneers understand this and work hard to make their defense the best in the **National Football League (NFL)**.

This book tells the story of the Buccaneers. They became a championship team in 2002, thanks to a defense that gave opponents no room to breathe. As that season showed, the Bucs win when everyone on the roster makes a contribution. Football is a lot of fun to watch when a team plays this way—and victory always seems a little sweeter.

Kellen Winslow Jr. gives quarterback Josh Freeman a tap of encouragement. The Bucs pull for one another in good times and bad.

THE MAGAZINE OF THE NATIONAL FOOTBALL LEAGUE

NOVEMBER 1981

pro!

Sid Gillman's
Anatomy of a
Game Plan

Territorial Rights:
Photo Essay on
Defensive Backs

Tex Schramm:
Power Behind
the Cowboys

The Redskin
as Cop

1981 Comebacks

NFL

Doug Williams
and Vince Evans:
Just Call Them
Quarterbacks

Tampa Bay's
Doug Williams

Football has a proud history in Florida. College and high school teams have been popular there for a long time. However, fans in the Sunshine State were introduced to **_professional_** football only a few **_decades_** ago. The first team to make an impact there was the Miami Dolphins. They began in the 1960s. By the 1970s, football fans on the opposite side of the state wanted their own team. In 1976, they got their wish. The Tampa Bay Buccaneers were born.

New teams usually have a hard time winning in the NFL, but no team ever had it harder than the Buccaneers. They lost all 14 of their games in 1976 and their first 12 in 1977. People started calling them the "Yuccaneers" and the "Bad News Bucs." Fortunately, Tampa Bay fans had the last laugh. In 1979, the Buccaneers won the **Central Division** of the **National Football Conference (NFC)** and nearly reached the **Super Bowl**.

Coach John McKay built a rock-solid defense with young stars such as brothers Lee Roy and Dewey Selmon, Dave Pear, Dave Lewis, and Richard Wood. Tampa Bay's leader on offense was Doug Williams, a strong-armed quarterback who never backed down from a challenge. Running back Ricky Bell and tight end Jimmie Giles were also important contributors. After their great 1979 season, the Buccaneers returned to the **playoffs** in 1981 and 1982.

In 1983, Williams signed a contract to play in the new **United States Football League (USFL)**. The Bucs struggled to find a new leader. For 14 seasons in a row, the team lost more games than it won. Many talented players wore the Tampa Bay uniform during this time, including James Wilder, Mark Carrier, Reggie Cobb, Steve Young, Vinny Testaverde, Ricky Reynolds, and Errict Rhett. Unfortunately, the Buccaneers couldn't find the winning *formula*.

In 1996, the team hired coach Tony Dungy. He went to work on rebuilding the Tampa Bay defense. Dungy assembled a group

LEFT: Doug Williams made front-page news with the Bucs in the 1970s.
ABOVE: James Wilder led the team in the 1980s.

of hard-hitting stars that included Hardy Nickerson, Derrick Brooks, John Lynch, and Warren Sapp. They made the fans forget about all of the team's disappointing years and instead remember the old days when the Bucs had the most fearsome defense in the NFL.

In 1997, Tampa Bay returned to the playoffs. The defense attacked opponents from all angles. On offense, running backs Mike Alstott and Warrick Dunn fueled a great rushing attack. Trent Dilfer threw 21 touchdown passes and rarely made a mistake. In December of that year, the Bucs won their first playoff game in nearly two decades.

As the Buccaneers added more quality players—including Brad Johnson, Keyshawn Johnson, Ronde Barber, Anthony McFarland, Simeon Rice, and Dexter Jackson—they made the **postseason** year after year. But the team needed a new spark to get to the Super Bowl. In 2002, the Bucs hired Jon Gruden to be their coach.

LEFT: Derrick Brooks keeps a watchful eye on a Tampa Bay opponent.
ABOVE: Ronde Barber and Warren Sapp

He was known as an offensive genius. Tampa Bay quickly rose to the top of the NFL.

In Gruden's first season, the Bucs went 12–4 and won the **NFC South**. They were even better in the playoffs. After two *lopsided* victories, Tampa Bay faced the Oakland Raiders in Super Bowl XXXVII. The game was never close. The Buccaneers cruised to a 48–21 win and their first championship.

In the years that followed, the Bucs and their fans discovered that winning the Super Bowl is often easier than repeating as champions. After several seasons, Tampa Bay started a new rebuilding effort. The team found exciting players such as running back Carnell "Cadillac" Williams, receivers Michael Clayton and Dave Moore, and linemen Donald Penn and Davin Joseph. They also relied on *veterans* such as Earnest Graham, Ike Hilliard, Joey Galloway, and Jeff Garcia.

The team's defense continued to shine under Barber and Brooks. They were joined by new stars, including pass-rusher Gaines Adams and defensive back Aqib Talib.

After a disappointing 3–13 record in 2009, the Bucs regrouped and began focusing on their future. They made young Josh Freeman their starting quarterback. He was big and strong, and his teammates were *inspired* by his desire to win. Freeman got help on offense from tight end Kellen Winslow Jr. and running back LeGarrette Blount. The defense welcomed new leaders, including Gerald McCoy, Sean Jones, and Adrian Clayborn.

In 2010, Freeman led one of history's youngest teams to within one victory of the playoffs. With a "changing of the guard" in full swing, the Buccaneers were ready to move into an exciting future by building on their proud past.

LEFT: Cadillac WIlliams looks for running room.
ABOVE: Aqib Talib takes a break during a Tampa Bay practice.

Home Turf

For their first 22 years, the Buccaneers played in Tampa Stadium. Some fans called the stadium the "Big Sombrero" because its shape reminded them of a Mexican hat. The Buccaneers moved into a new stadium in 1998. It is roomy and comfortable for the fans, and NFL players love the grass playing surface.

One of the challenges faced by the Bucs is keeping the field dry during Florida rainstorms. The team makes sure that it's always ready for bad weather. The Bucs also do a good job entertaining their fans. Their favorite part of the stadium is Buccaneer Cove. Located behind the north end zone, it features a 103-foot *replica* of a pirate ship.

BY THE NUMBERS

- The Bucs' stadium has 65,857 seats.
- The stadium has two video screens. Each is 24 feet tall and 92 feet wide.
- The replica pirate ship weighs 43 tons.

The famous pirate ship can be seen behind the north end zone.

Dressed for Success

In their early years, the Buccaneers had some of the most recognizable uniforms in the NFL. The team's first colors were red, white, and bright orange. The Buccaneers wore white pants with orange tops, or orange pants with white tops. Coach Sam Wyche once asked the players to wear orange pants and tops at the same time. Hardy Nickerson, the team's star linebacker, told him to forget it!

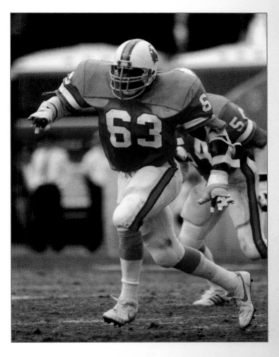

In 1997, the Buccaneers changed their team colors to red, black, orange, and a metallic color called pewter. Tampa Bay also changed its *logo* from a pirate in a fancy hat to the famous skull and crossed swords. The fans love the team's look. They proudly wear Tampa Bay's colors to every home game.

LEFT: Josh Freeman warms up in the team's 2011 road uniform.
ABOVE: Lee Roy Selmon wears Tampa Bay's old home uniform.

15

D oes an NFL team need a superstar to win the Super Bowl? Tampa Bay fans asked that question as the 2002 season began. The Buccaneers had a talented roster, but most of their players were not well-known to football fans outside of Florida. In fact, no one made more headlines than coach Jon Gruden. Many people

considered him the best coach in the league. Before the season, Tampa Bay sent four **draft** picks and $8 million to the Oakland Raiders to get him.

Gruden took over a team with a ***dominant*** defense. Warren Sapp controlled the **line of scrimmage**. Simeon Rice was a nightmare for opposing quarterbacks. Derrick Brooks and John Lynch roamed all over the field to make tackles. Ronde Barber, Brian Kelly, and Dexter Jackson made passing against the Bucs very dangerous. In the 2002 regular

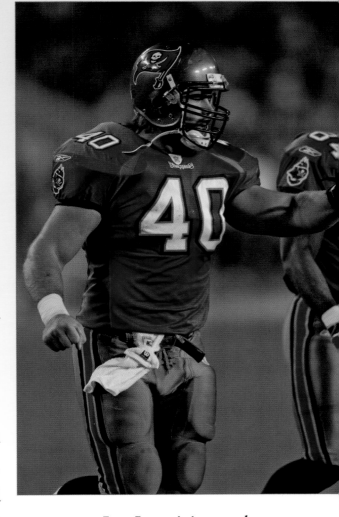

season, Tampa Bay allowed just 196 points in 16 games.

The Buccaneers won the NFC South with a record of 12–4. However, they got bad news when quarterback Brad Johnson went down with an injury. He had thrown for 22 touchdowns before getting hurt. Would he be healthy in the playoffs? No one knew for sure.

Tampa Bay opened the postseason against the San Francisco 49ers. Johnson took the field and looked great. In the first half, he tossed scoring passes to Joe Jurevicius and Rickey Dudley. The rushing attack was also working. Mike Alstott blasted into the end zone on two short runs.

Meanwhile, the Tampa Bay defense pounded San Francisco quarterback Jeff Garcia. They sacked him four times and forced the 49ers into five **turnovers**. The Bucs won easily, 31–6.

Next, they traveled to Philadelphia to play the Eagles in the **NFC Championship Game**. Most of the experts predicted a win by the Eagles. The weather forecast for Philadelphia was freezing cold and wet. In their entire history, the Bucs had won only one game in these conditions. Even worse, they had lost in the playoffs two years in a row to the Eagles.

Things looked bad when Philadelphia scored in the first minute of the game. True to form, the Tampa Bay defense tightened up. The offense also found its rhythm. Alstott ran for a touchdown in the first quarter. Brad Johnson hit Keyshawn Johnson for a touchdown in the second quarter. Martin Gramatica added two **field goals** for a 20–10 lead.

With the Eagles driving deep into Tampa Bay territory in the fourth quarter, Barber made the play of the game. He intercepted a

pass and ran it back 92 yards for a touchdown. The Buccaneers were NFC champions for the first time.

In Super Bowl XXXVII, Tampa Bay faced Gruden's old team, the Raiders. He knew exactly what to expect from Oakland and spent a week preparing his players for everything the Raiders would try. The Buccaneers proved to be great students. The defense intercepted five passes and returned three for touchdowns. Johnson threw for two touchdowns, and Alstott ran for one. Gramatica kicked two field goals to make the final score 48–21.

In their 27th season, the Bucs were champions of football. Safety Dexter Jackson was named the game's **Most Valuable Player (MVP)**. It was just the third time ever that a defensive back won the award.

LEFT: Ronde Barber watches the action from the Tampa Bay sidelines.
ABOVE: Dexter Jackson takes off with one of his two interceptions during Super Bowl XXXVII.

To be a true star in the NFL, you need more than fast feet and a big body. You have to be a "go-to guy"—someone the coach wants on the field at the end of a big game. Buccaneers fans have had a lot to cheer about over the years, including these great stars …

THE PIONEERS

LEE ROY SELMON   Defensive Lineman

- BORN: 10/20/1954   • DIED: 9/4/2011   • PLAYED FOR TEAM: 1976 TO 1984

Lee Roy Selmon could do it all—fight off big offensive linemen, tackle fast running backs, and sack the quarterback. From 1979 to 1984, he was the top defensive end in the league. Selmon's older brother, Dewey, was also a defensive star for Tampa Bay.

JIMMIE GILES   Tight End

- BORN: 11/8/1954   • PLAYED FOR TEAM: 1978 TO 1986

Jimmie Giles was big and fast with sure hands. He once scored four touchdowns in a game against the Miami Dolphins. Giles caught the winning touchdown in the 1986 **Pro Bowl**.

DOUG WILLIAMS   Quarterback

- BORN: 8/9/1955   • PLAYED FOR TEAM: 1978 TO 1982

Doug Williams had a cannon for a right arm. He was also a great leader who inspired his teammates to play their best. In 1979, Williams guided the Bucs to their first appearance in the NFC Championship Game.

JAMES WILDER   Running Back

- BORN: 5/12/1958   • PLAYED FOR TEAM: 1981 TO 1989

James Wilder was as tough as nails. Instead of running around tacklers, he preferred to run them over. Wilder was an **All-Pro** in 1984 when he rushed for 1,544 yards and 13 touchdowns.

HARDY NICKERSON   Linebacker

- BORN: 9/1/1965   • PLAYED FOR TEAM: 1993 TO 1999

Hardy Nickerson was so *intense* during games that teammates nicknamed him the "Dragon." He made tackles all over the field. Nickerson played in the Pro Bowl five times with the Bucs.

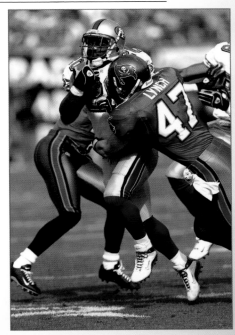

JOHN LYNCH   Defensive Back

- BORN: 9/25/1971   • PLAYED FOR TEAM: 1993 TO 2003

John Lynch was the hardest-hitting safety in the NFL. He caused opponents to think twice about catching a pass in the middle of the field. Lynch was named All-Pro twice.

LEFT: Jimmie Giles
RIGHT: John Lynch takes down a runner.

DERRICK BROOKS   Linebacker

- BORN: 4/18/1973   • PLAYED FOR TEAM: 1995 TO 2008

Derrick Brooks spent 14 seasons with Tampa Bay. No one was more feared on the field or more respected off it. In the team's championship season, Brooks was the NFL Defensive Player of the Year.

WARREN SAPP   Defensive Lineman

- BORN: 12/19/1972   • PLAYED FOR TEAM: 1995 TO 2003

Warren Sapp had amazing speed and quickness for a player his size. Opponents often had to use two blockers on him, and he still could break free and make a tackle. Sapp was named All-Pro six seasons in a row starting in 1997.

MIKE ALSTOTT   Running Back

- BORN: 12/21/1973   • PLAYED FOR TEAM: 1996 TO 2006

Mike Alstott was a powerful runner who was even more dangerous as the lead blocker for Warrick Dunn. He played in the Pro Bowl every year from 1997 to 2002. Alstott scored the first touchdown of Super Bowl XXXVII.

RONDE BARBER   Defensive Back

- BORN: 4/7/1975   • FIRST YEAR WITH TEAM: 1997

Nothing could slow down Ronde Barber—not even "Father Time." After 15 seasons—all with the Bucs—he was still going strong. Barber was the first cornerback in NFL history to have 20 sacks and 20 interceptions in his career.

AQIB TALIB   Defensive Back

- BORN: 2/13/1986   • FIRST YEAR WITH TEAM: 2008

Aqib Talib was just the second defensive back that the Bucs ever picked in the first round of the draft. In 2008, he led all **rookies** in interceptions. In 2009, Talib intercepted three passes in one game. In 2011, he returned two interceptions for touchdowns.

JOSH FREEMAN   Quarterback

- BORN: 1/13/1988   • FIRST YEAR WITH TEAM: 2009

Josh Freeman reminded some fans of Doug Williams. Both were blessed with a great arm and terrific leadership skills. In just his second season, Freeman threw 22 touchdown passes and guided the Bucs to a 10-6 record. The following year, he ran for four scores.

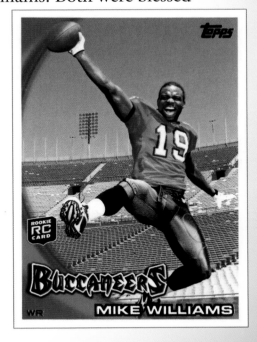

MIKE WILLIAMS   Receiver

- BORN: 5/18/1987   • FIRST YEAR WITH TEAM: 2010

Mike Williams became an NFL star as a rookie. That season, he led all first-year receivers with 65 catches and set a team record with 11 touchdowns. Williams combined with Kellen Winslow Jr. to give Tampa Bay a great one-two punch in the passing game.

LEFT: Derrick Brooks
RIGHT: Mike Williams

Calling the Shots

Because of Florida's proud football history, coaching the Bucs is a great challenge that brings lots of pressure. Some of the NFL's most respected leaders have worked on the sidelines for the Buccaneers, including Leeman Bennett, Ray Perkins, and Sam Wyche. The team's first coach was John McKay. Before he joined the Buccaneers, he won four national championships in college at the University of Southern California. McKay took the Bucs from a winless season to the NFC Championship Game in just three years. He was known for his sense of humor. Even when the Bucs lost, he gave fans something to smile about.

Tony Dungy coached Tampa Bay from 1996 to 2001. He was a very nice man who *motivated* his players by constantly encouraging them to work hard and play their best. Dungy built one of the

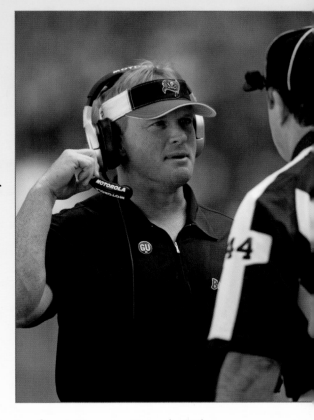

NFL's top defenses and led the team to the playoffs four times. Jon Gruden took over for Dungy in 2002. He was one of the NFL's youngest and most intense coaches. He lived and breathed football and expected the same from his players.

There was great pressure on Gruden to win a championship. He didn't mind at all. In Gruden's first season with the Bucs, they won 12 games and rolled through the postseason to advance to their first Super Bowl. The Buccaneers crushed the Oakland Raiders, 48–21. Tampa Bay fans and players gave credit to Gruden and Dungy for the amazing victory. Gruden's game plan worked to perfection, and the swarming defense that Dungy had built accounted for half of the team's six touchdowns.

In 2012, the Buccaneers hired Greg Schiano. He had been one of the best coaches in college football. The Bucs were confident that he would work the same magic in his first NFL coaching job.

One Great Day

No coach in the NFL took more care preparing for a game than Jon Gruden. He was even more focused than usual as the Buccaneers got ready for Super Bowl XXXVII against the Oakland Raiders. Gruden was very familiar with his opponent. He had coached the Raiders for four seasons before taking over the Bucs.

Gruden left nothing to chance. He put together a game plan that would destroy the high-scoring Raiders. As the game started, his

players felt extremely confident. They knew the Oakland playbook as well as the Raiders did.

The Bucs allowed three points early in the first quarter. After that, the Tampa Bay defense smothered the Raiders. Dexter Jackson intercepted two passes to stop Oakland scoring drives. Dwight Smith also had two interceptions and returned both for touchdowns. Derrick Brooks ran back an interception for a score, too.

Meanwhile, the Buccaneers moved the ball up and down the field against the Oakland defense. Michael Pittman rushed for 124 yards, Brad Johnson threw for two touchdowns, and Keyshawn Johnson caught six passes. The final score was 48–21. Jackson was voted the game's MVP.

Afterward, everyone watching agreed that no team had ever been better prepared than the Bucs for the Super Bowl. John Lynch said it best: "I've never been involved in a game where everything we ran in practice played out so identically."

Legend Has It

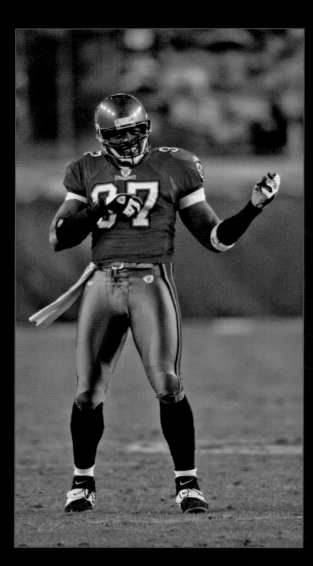

Are the Buccaneers the masters of the quarterback sack?

LEGEND HAS IT that they are. From the days of the Selmon brothers until now, the Tampa Bay defense has struck fear into the hearts of NFL passers. The Bucs once set a record by sacking the quarterback in 69 games in a row. No one had more fun pressuring opposing passers than Simeon Rice. In his first five seasons in Tampa Bay, he had 67.5 sacks. Rice even wrote a book about his life as a "sack master" called *Rush to Judgment*.

ABOVE: Simeon Rice celebrates a sack with an "air guitar" solo.
RIGHT: Dave Pear

Who was the team's best wrestler?

LEGEND HAS IT that Errict Rhett was. In fact, Rhett was a national champion in high school. With all of that experience pinning opponents to the mat, Rhett would have made a good blocker or defender. Instead, he became a running back. "Wrestling taught me *coordination* and balance," he once said. "Wrestling helped me break tackles and keep moving."

Which Buccaneer fought hardest for his fellow NFL players?

LEGEND HAS IT that Dave Pear did. Pear played on the defensive line for the Bucs. In 1979, he became the first player in team history to go to the Pro Bowl. After retiring from the NFL, Pear began to feel the ill effects of his career in football. He started a *blog* that educated people about the many injuries suffered by NFL players. To this day, Pear fights for the rights of disabled players.

As the 1976 NFL season began, Tampa Bay fans weren't exactly sure what to expect from their team. The Buccaneers were new to the league and had very few experienced players. To make matters worse, the NFL had placed the Bucs in the **American Football Conference (AFC)**. (The following year, the Bucs would move to the NFC.) Their **division** was one of the best in football. The Oakland Raiders, Denver Broncos, San Diego Chargers, and Kansas City Chiefs were all good teams. The poor Bucs had to face each of them—twice!

Tampa Bay's quarterback was Steve Spurrier. He had been a college superstar in Florida, so he was a familiar face to the fans. Unfortunately, nothing prepared him to lead this struggling team. In five games during the 1976 season, the Buccaneers failed to score a single point. Tampa Bay reached 20 points only once, against the mighty Miami Dolphins. Even then, the Bucs lost. The Dolphins kicked a field goal in the fourth quarter for a 23–20 victory.

That loss actually gave Tampa Bay fans some hope. It showed that the team had the makings of a strong defense. Young stars

Steve Spurrier drops back to pass. His first year with the Bucs
was also his last as an NFL quarterback.

Lee Roy and Dewey Selmon were the leaders of the unit. The Bucs
caused 28 turnovers during the season. Mark Cotney led the way with
three interceptions.

However, good defense was not enough for the Buccaneers in their
first season. They went the entire year without a win. The team's
record of 0–14 made history. Surprisingly, many fans think fondly
of that year. For all their mistakes and losses, the Bucs never gave up.
That same attitude was a big reason Tampa Bay made it to the NFC
Championship Game three seasons later.

Team Spirit

When the Buccaneers play a home game, the cities of Tampa and St. Petersburg come alive. Fans dress in red, pack the stadium, and scream as loud as they can. They try to distract the other team with their cheers and let the Bucs know that they appreciate a full effort.

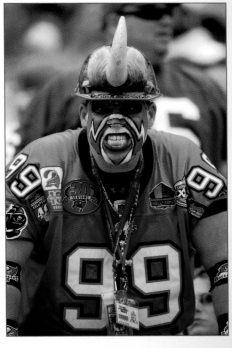

The players always give their best. The Tampa Bay fans accept nothing less. They have stuck with the team through all its ups and downs, always staying loyal to the Bucs.

There's plenty to do and see at the stadium on game day. When the Bucs move the ball close to the goal line, red flags are raised up the flagpoles surrounding the upper deck. After the team scores, the pirate ship in Buccaneer Cove fires fun prizes from its cannons. When the song "Yo Ho (A Pirate's Life for Me)" plays, fans sing along.

LEFT: Flag-toting cheerleaders get the crowd on its feet.
ABOVE: This fan would scare a real buccaneer!

Timeline

In this timeline, each Super Bowl is listed under the year it was played. Remember that the Super Bowl is held early in the year and is actually part of the previous season. For example, Super Bowl XLVI was played on February 5, 2012, but it was the championship of the 2011 NFL season.

1976
The Bucs play their first season.

1984
James Wilder sets an NFL record with 407 carries.

1979
The Bucs reach the playoffs for the first time.

1987
The Bucs take Vinny Testaverde first in the draft.

1994
Errict Rhett rushes for 1,000 yards as a rookie.

Ricky Bell was the team's top runner in 1979.

Vinny Testaverde

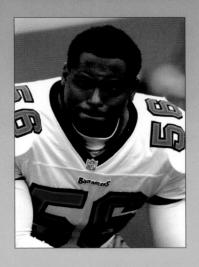

Hardy Nickerson was an All-Pro in 1997.

Jeff Garcia

1997
The Bucs return to the playoffs.

2003
The Bucs win Super Bowl XXXVII.

2007
Jeff Garcia plays in the Pro Bowl.

2001
Keyshawn Johnson sets a team record with 106 catches.

2005
Cadillac Williams is named Offensive Rookie of the Year.

2010
LeGarrette Blount runs for more than 1,000 yards.

Keyshawn Johnson

Fun Facts

COMEBACK KIDS

In 1980, Doug Williams led the Bucs to five fourth-quarter comeback victories. In 2010, Josh Freeman matched Williams's team record.

IN THE TRENCHES

One of Tampa Bay's most popular players was David Logan. He played on the defensive line in the 1980s, often going up against blockers who outweighed him by 50 to 100 pounds. After he retired from football, Logan became a popular broadcaster for the Bucs.

LAST BUT NOT LEAST

Aqib Talib's first name means "the last one" in Arabic. His mother gave him that name because he was the youngest of her four children.

ABOVE: David Logan
RIGHT: Matt Bryant

LONG RANGE

In 2006, Matt Bryant beat the Philadelphia Eagles with a 62-yard field goal. It was the second-longest field goal in NFL history.

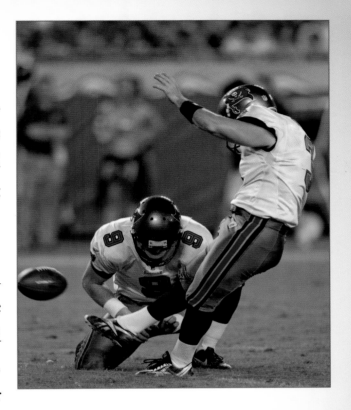

NAME GAME

The Buccaneers got their name from a contest. Fans submitted their ideas, and "Buccaneers" won. A buccaneer is another name for a pirate. Each February, the city of Tampa holds a Gasparilla Pirate Festival. It has been a *tradition* since 1904.

BRAVE HEART

Ricky Bell was Tampa Bay's first great running back. He rushed for 1,263 yards in 1979. Bell played despite having a rare heart disease. He died in 1984. Later, there was a movie made about Bell's life called *A Triumph of the Heart.*

Talking Football

"One is to make a name for yourself. Two is to stick around long enough to make a little money. Three is to win a championship. I've done all three of those."

► **Ronde Barber,** *on his three goals as an NFL player*

"Any success I've had is the result of my play and my passion for the game I love."

► **John Lynch,** *on what football means to him*

"Just being around him you feel energy. You hand him the ball, you think good things are going to happen."

► **Jon Gruden,** *on Cadillac Williams*

"I was able to make the other guys on the team believe in me and believe in themselves. That was very satisfying to me."

► **Doug Williams,** *on the team's great season in 1979*

"You never know who's going to be good, who's going to win. It comes down to making plays on Sunday."

▶ **Josh Freeman,** *on the importance of preparing well for each game*

"He's a playmaker and the type of guy who's always around the football. You just have to look where the football is and you'll find him."

▶ **Jeff Garcia,** *on Derrick Brooks*

"The Eagles didn't know what hit them. They really expected to win this game, and we were beating them up on every play."

▶ **Simeon Rice,** *on the 2002 NFC Championship Game*

LEFT: Ronde Barber
ABOVE: Josh Freeman

Great Debates

People who root for the Buccaneers love to compare their favorite moments, teams, and players. Some debates have been going on for years! How would you settle these classic football arguments?

The 2002 Bucs would beat the 1979 Bucs ....

... because their defense was just too good. When the Bucs took the field on defense in 2002, they didn't just expect to stop the other team. They expected to score points! The Bucs had five defensive touchdowns that season—four were scored by Derrick Brooks. Simeon Rice also had a sack in the end zone for another two points. In Super Bowl XXXVII, the Bucs scored three more touchdowns on defense!

Not so fast. The 1979 Bucs would hold their own ....

DEWEY SELMON

BUCCANEERS

LB

... because they were a tough team that never gave up. Doug Williams would outrun the 2002 pass rush. Jimmie Giles would keep the linebackers busy, while Ricky Bell would pick up first downs running the football. Plus, don't forget about the Tampa Bay defense in 1979. Brothers Lee Roy and Dewey Selmon (LEFT) led a unit that stopped opponents cold.

Warren Sapp was Tampa Bay's greatest defensive player …

… because no one caused more *mayhem* on a football field. Sapp was fast and powerful. He also had a "let's get crazy" attitude, which set him apart from every other player at his position. Sapp was like a brick wall when teams tried to run through the Tampa Bay line. But he was also a great pass-rusher. In fact, only one defensive tackle in history had more quarterback sacks.

No way. Derrick Brooks wins this argument …

… because he was the best linebacker in the NFC for 15 years. Brooks (RIGHT) and Sapp were drafted by the Bucs the same year. However, Brooks was the leader of the defense. Look at the 2002 championship season. Brooks scored four touchdowns. Three came on interception returns—no linebacker had ever done that before. In Super Bowl XXXVII, Brooks sealed Tampa Bay's victory when he intercepted a pass and ran it in for his fifth touchdown that year.

T he great Buccaneers teams and players have left their marks on the record books. These are the "best of the best" …

Warrick Dunn

Warren Sapp

BUCCANEERS AWARD WINNERS

WINNER	AWARD	YEAR
Lee Roy Selmon	Defensive Player of the Year	1979
Lee Roy Selmon	Pro Bowl Defensive MVP	1982
Warrick Dunn	Offensive Rookie of the Year	1997
Warren Sapp	Defensive Player of the Year	1999
Derrick Brooks	Defensive Player of the Year	2002
Dexter Jackson	Super Bowl XXXVII MVP	2003
Cadillac Williams	Offensive Rookie of the Year	2005
Derrick Brooks	Pro Bowl MVP	2006

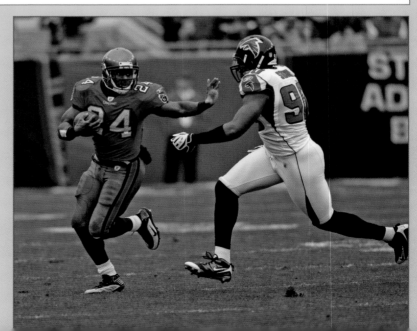

Cadillac Williams

BUCCANEERS ACHIEVEMENTS

ACHIEVEMENT	YEAR
NFC Central Champions	1979
NFC Champions	1979
NFC Central Champions	1981
NFC Central Champions	1999
NFC South Champions	2002
NFC Champions	2002
Super Bowl XXXVII Champions	2002*
NFC South Champions	2005
NFC South Champions	2007

Super Bowls are played early the following year, but the game is counted as the championship of this season.

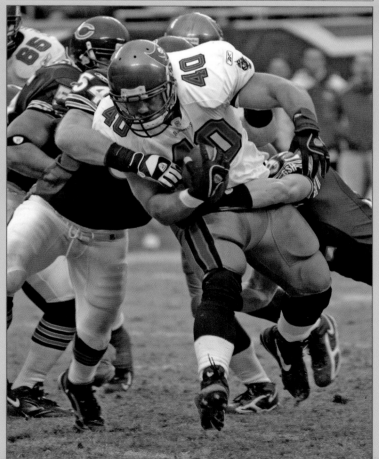

ABOVE: Simeon Rice led the 2002 team with 15.5 sacks.
LEFT: Mike Alstott was an All-Pro in 1999.

Pinpoints

The history of a football team is made up of many smaller stories. These stories take place all over the map—not just in the city a team calls "home." Match the pushpins on these maps to the **Team Facts**, and you will begin to see the story of the Buccaneers unfold!

TEAM FACTS

1 Tampa, Florida—*The team has played here since 1976.*

2 Pensacola, Florida—*Derrick Brooks was born here.*

3 Roanoke, Virginia—*Ronde Barber was born here.*

4 Knoxville, Tennessee—*Reggie Cobb was born here.*

5 Marietta, Georgia—*Brad Johnson was born here.*

6 Zachary, Louisiana—*Doug Williams was born here.*

7 Kansas City, Missouri—*Josh Freeman was born here.*

8 Joliet, Illinois—*Mike Alstott was born here.*

9 Houston, Texas—*Ricky Bell was born here.*

10 Eufaula, Oklahoma—*Lee Roy and Dewey Selmon were born here.*

11 San Diego, California—*The Bucs won Super Bowl XXXVII here.*

12 Buenos Aires, Argentina—*Martin Gramatica was born here.*

Martin Gramatica

Glossary

🧠 **ALL-PRO**—An honor given to the best players at their positions at the end of each season.

🧠 **AMERICAN FOOTBALL CONFERENCE (AFC)**—One of two groups of teams that make up the NFL.

🧠 *BLOG*—A list of journal entries posted on a web page—short for "Web Log."

🧠 **CENTRAL DIVISION**—A group of teams that play in the central part of the country.

🧠 *COORDINATION*—The ability to effectively use all body parts at the same time.

🧠 *DECADES*—Periods of 10 years; also specific periods, such as the 1950s.

🧠 **DIVISION**—A group of teams that play in the same part of the country.

🧠 *DOMINANT*—Ruling or controlling.

🧠 **DRAFT**—The annual meeting during which NFL teams choose from a group of the best college players.

🧠 **FIELD GOALS**—Goals from the field, kicked over the crossbar and between the goal posts. A field goal is worth three points.

🧠 *FORMULA*—A set way of doing something.

🧠 *INSPIRED*—Received positive and confident feelings.

🧠 *INTENSE*—Extremely strong or serious.

🧠 **INTERCEPTIONS**—Passes that are caught by the defensive team.

🧠 **LINE OF SCRIMMAGE**—The imaginary line that separates the offense and defense before each play begins.

🧠 *LOGO*—A symbol or design that represents a company or team.

🧠 *LOPSIDED*—Extremely uneven.

🧠 *MAYHEM*—Trouble or chaos.

🧠 **MOST VALUABLE PLAYER (MVP)**—The award given each year to the league's best player; also given to the best player in the Super Bowl and Pro Bowl.

🧠 *MOTIVATED*—Inspired to achieve.

🧠 **NATIONAL FOOTBALL CONFERENCE (NFC)**—One of two groups of teams that make up the NFL.

🧠 **NATIONAL FOOTBALL LEAGUE (NFL)**—The league that started in 1920 and is still operating today.

🧠 **NFC CHAMPIONSHIP GAME**—The game played to determine which NFC team will go to the Super Bowl.

🧠 **NFC SOUTH**—A division for teams that play in the southern part of the country.

🧠 **PLAYOFFS**—The games played after the regular season to determine which teams play in the Super Bowl.

🧠 **POSTSEASON**—Another term for playoffs.

🧠 **PRO BOWL**—The NFL's all-star game, played after the regular season.

🧠 *PROFESSIONAL*—Paid to play.

🧠 *REPLICA*—Exact copy.

🧠 **ROOKIES**—Players in their first year.

🧠 **SACKS**—Tackles of the quarterback behind the line of scrimmage.

🧠 **SUPER BOWL**—The championship of the NFL, played between the winners of the National Football Conference and American Football Conference.

🧠 *TRADITION*—A belief or custom that is handed down from generation to generation.

🧠 **TURNOVERS**—Fumbles or interceptions that give the ball to the other team.

🧠 **UNITED STATES FOOTBALL LEAGUE (USFL)**—The league that tried to challenge the NFL in the 1980s. The USFL started in 1983 and ended in 1985.

🧠 **VETERANS**—Players with great experience.

OVERTIME

TEAM SPIRIT introduces a great way to stay up to date with your team! Visit our **OVERTIME** link and get connected to the latest and greatest updates. **OVERTIME** serves as a young reader's ticket to an exclusive web page—with more stories, fun facts, team records, and photos of the Buccaneers. Content is updated during and after each season. The **OVERTIME** feature also enables readers to send comments and letters to the author! Log onto:

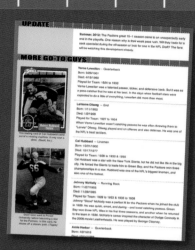

www.norwoodhousepress.com/library.aspx

and click on the tab: **TEAM SPIRIT** to access **OVERTIME**.

Read all the books in the series to learn more about professional sports. For a complete listing of the baseball, basketball, football, and hockey teams in the **TEAM SPIRIT** series, visit our website at:

www.norwoodhousepress.com/library.aspx

On the Road

TAMPA BAY BUCCANEERS
One Buccaneer Place
Tampa, Florida 33607
813- 870-2700
www.buccaneers.com

THE PRO FOOTBALL HALL OF FAME
2121 George Halas Drive NW
Canton, Ohio 44708
330-456-8207
www.profootballhof.com

On the Bookshelf

To learn more about the sport of football, look for these books at your library or bookstore:

- Frederick, Shane. *The Best of Everything Football Book.* North Mankato, Minnesota: Capstone Press, 2011.

- Jacobs, Greg. *The Everything Kids' Football Book: The All-Time Greats, Legendary Teams, Today's Superstars—And Tips on Playing Like a Pro.* Avon, Massachusetts: Adams Media Corporation, 2010.

- Editors of *Sports Illustrated for Kids. 1st and 10: Top 10 Lists of Everything in Football.* New York, New York: Sports Illustrated Books, 2011.

Index

PAGE NUMBERS IN **BOLD** REFER TO ILLUSTRATIONS.

About the Author

MARK STEWART has written more than 50 books on football and over 150 sports books for kids. He grew up in New York City during the 1960s rooting for the Giants and Jets, and was lucky enough to meet players from both teams. Mark comes from a family of writers. His grandfather was Sunday Editor of *The New York Times,* and his mother was Articles Editor of *Ladies' Home Journal* and *McCall's.* Mark has profiled hundreds of athletes over the past 25 years. He has also written several books about his native New York and New Jersey, his home today. Mark is a graduate of Duke University, with a degree in history. He lives and works in a home overlooking Sandy Hook, New Jersey. You can contact Mark through the Norwood House Press website.

ML   10-15